IT STARTED WITH A DREAM

How to Find Your Dream

Catherine Scott

Trilogy Christian Publishers
A Wholly Owned Subsidiary of Trinity Broadcasting Network
2442 Michelle Drive
Tustin, CA 92780
Copyright © 2021 by Catherine Scott
All Scripture quotations, unless otherwise noted, taken from
THE HOLY BIBLE, NEW INTERNATIONAL VERSION®,
NIV® Copyright © 1973, 1978, 1984, 2011 by Biblica, Inc.®
Used by permission. All rights reserved worldwide.
Scripture quotations marked (KJV) taken from The Holy Bible, King James Version. Cambridge Edition: 1769.
All rights reserved, including the right to reproduce this book or portions thereof in any form whatsoever.
For information, address Trilogy Christian Publishing
Rights Department, 2442 Michelle Drive, Tustin, Ca 92780.
Trilogy Christian Publishing/ TBN and colophon are trademarks of Trinity Broadcasting Network.
For information about special discounts for bulk purchases, please contact Trilogy Christian Publishing.
Manufactured in the United States of America

10 9 8 7 6 5 4 3 2 1
Library of Congress Cataloging-in-Publication Data is available.
ISBN 978-1-64773-811-2
ISBN 978-1-64773-812-9 (ebook)

Dedication

To Bill and Bonnie Lambley, our parents who taught us so much.

With love and appreciation from their children; Carol, Catherine, Connie, Christine, and "Sweet Craig William"

Acknowledgments

There are not words enough to thank my totally awesome sons: Dale, Clint, and Justin Burr Scott. I literally could not have made it without all your support through the years.

Then, of course, there are Kim, Lauren, and Aman, my three strong, kind, beautiful "daughters." You are true treasures to me.

Last, but certainly not least, I thank God for Courtney and Andrew, Cole, Cameron, Dylan, Caroline, Ava, Mia, Layla, and Travis. I carry you all in my heart, always.

Where would we be without prayer? Kudos to Judy Crow for always praying me through, and Pat Deweese Woods for listening to all of us!

A big thank you to Charlotte Guevara for your generous, caring heart. Without you, this book would not have happened.

Appreciations

"It did not take me long to realize I had met a very special woman seventeen years ago. Catherine is not only a woman that uses her special relationship with God to do good for friends and community. She knows when someone needs a phone call or a visit. Just when you need her, she is there. What I love about her is she never judges or pushes her beliefs; she just lives them. She helps you see how God is always walking with you even if you don't realize it at the time. She listens to God and reaches out to help those who need His help. Catherine loves everyone, even those who are hard to love. She lives her faith and shares God through her love. Yes, a very special woman, indeed. A woman I am proud to call my friend."

Major Nancy Crouse
Colonel Craig McCurdy

"In our lives, we have had many mentors, friends, and caregivers, and Catherine represents the best in all those areas. She really cares about people, she is non-judgmental, and has an inner-intuitive skill that allows her to say the right thing at the right time to help the human condition."

Dr. Jean Holden, Ph.D.
Dr. Orbry Holden, Ph.D.

"Catherine has been our friend for twenty-two years. We have witnessed her first-hand in her ministry of caring for people as she shows them how the Lord is working in their lives."

Jim and Maggie Taliano
Fisher Porter, V.P.

TABLE OF CONTENTS

Prologue.. 11

Foreword.. 13

Chapter 1.. 17

Chapter 2.. 21

Chapter 3.. 25

Chapter 4.. 31

Chapter 5.. 35

Chapter 6.. 41

Chapter 7.. 45

Chapter 8 49

Chapter 9.. 55

Chapter 10.. 61

Chapter 11 69

Chapter 12 75

Chapter 13 83

Chapter 14 87

It Started with a Dream 91

Biography 93

Prologue

If someone asked you to define or explain "spiritual gifts," as it pertains to Christianity, could you? I am sure most of us proclaimed followers of Christ and devoted readers of God's Word could at least provide some sort of explanation. As much as we might be able to explain and identify the different spiritual gifts given to each one of us by the Holy Spirit, could we list our gift, or gifts, with absolute certainty? If so, do we know what to do with them or even when to use them? We know that every Christian is given at least one spiritual gift that is to be used for the building up and edification of the church. But are we truly using our gift(s) for this purpose, no matter the consequences, to our life here on Earth? I know I have asked too many questions perhaps, but my goal is to have you think and prepare for what is to come in the following pages of this book.

The true stories that are presented in this book by Catherine are examples of God using an ordinary person to convey a message to someone or impact that person's life in a positive way. These stories are only possible and explained by first, Catherine understanding and accepting her God-given spiritual gift, and then being obedient to God in carrying out His will in these circumstances.

In no way is the intent of this book to raise Catherine to a higher level of importance than any other person within the church's body of believers. Instead, it is a book that can lift your faith and inspire Christians to pursue their own spiritual gifts no matter what they are. It certainly has done that for me.

And for those that have not yet found their way to believe in God and His Son, Jesus Christ, I would hope that the seed will be planted. I truly hope that you will not delay in accepting the most wonderful gift of all, God's grace, and join us as brothers and sisters in Christ.

Carl W. Lundgren

Foreword

By Jacque Heasley
Minister, Writer, Singer

In 1981, God spoke to me that if I would make him Lord of my life, I would sing all over the world. I began to see visions of immense crowds in Africa that I would be singing to. It seemed like an impossible task for a girl from Pampa, Texas. These visions persisted. I shared these visions with family and friends and they sometimes doubted me (Mark 6:4, NIV) A prophet is not without honor except in his own town, among his relatives and in his own home. They all know our human frailties. I knew God's voice.

In 1985, we moved to Terrell, Texas. I took a job as a legal secretary to David S. Mallard. David is a brilliant lawyer, a judge, a wonderfully honest person, and a supportive teacher. He encouraged everyone, and also me, in ministry. I worked at the law firm for three years. Then God started tugging at my heart that it was time to resign and prepare for the ministry He was calling me to. I saturated myself in the word and sat under a great teacher named Teddy Hunt.

Then, one average day, I was at work and a beautiful, young woman walked in. She did not have an appointment, she did not know anyone in the office, or even what type of office it was. She was quite timid as I asked her name and how I could help her. She said, "I am Catherine Scott, I don't know how you believe, and I don't know exactly why I am here, however, the Lord told me to bring my resume in here." She was a single mom with three sons, and she needed a different job. God was leading.

I quickly looked to the left and right and said, "How did you know I was leaving? I haven't told anyone yet. God is calling me into full-time ministry." Catherine reminded me she had no way of knowing that I was leaving. She was just listening to the Holy Spirit.

I quickly resigned, and through a process, Catherine replaced me. She, by the way, appreciated David as much as I did. It was amazing to see how God had spoken to both of us in such a powerful way and how we saw His hand maneuver our lives for His Glory. Yes, for many years, I did go to Africa and sing for those immense crowds.

Catherine and I became best of friends and have become like sisters. I love her dearly. I have seen God use Catherine miraculously so many times through the years. She truly has the ear of the Lord. Her book will inspire its readers.

1.

DARRELL

My awesome friend and faithful hairstylist, Darrell Kidd, and I got off to a bumpy start. I had been to see him once, and during my appointment, he let me know; if you were late, he would send you home and to come back later or not, was your choice. In conversation that first day, I thought Darrell was the big, tough military man he was and appeared to be. I am not very bold. I do tend to see the good in people, so, of course, I came back for a second appointment. This time, however, I had just seen a plane go down in which two men were killed and two burned very badly. I was there at the scene when one young wife and small children arrived at the scene.

I had just arrived and sat down for my second appointment. I was five minutes late and Darrel said "something" tough to me. I began to cry and pour out my story of the day before, and that on this day, I had to pull over because I was crying and that is why I was late. I was a blubbering mess, hurt to the core by what I witnessed; a man on fire, two dead, and fatherless little children asking for their Papa.

I quickly learned Darrell had a great, big heart and wasn't nearly as tough as he appeared. He brought me food, a drink, and Kleenex, etc., and apologized all the while. We became fast friends for what is now over twenty years. Thank you, BJ, for introducing me to Darrell.

Please understand, I am a very faulty, fragile, imperfect human being. The stories to follow are all to God's glory and obedience to Him. My life has actually been very simple and at the same time, complex. What I would like to accomplish in this book is to just convey the miracles the Lord has done through and for me, my sons, and others through the work of the Holy Spirit. To also encourage you to do the same through your gifts. We all need to be His hands and feet.

After all those years and many Christian discussions with Darrell, in January 2018, I went to see Darrell and he excitedly started telling me about a dream he had about me two nights before. Darrell's dream caught the very essence of who I am. In his dream, he said that everything around was a pure, filmy white. I had on a beautiful, filmy gown and I was being married (it sounded like a spiritual wedding). The flowers were white, and the surroundings were pure white. He painted a very ethereal picture. Darrell also said there was always a white light over me and that when I moved, the light moved, and I quote, "Like touched by an angel." He said in the dream, the Lord used me as an angel. He then asked me if that was true. I said, "Yes, that is exactly what I have spent my life doing." He asked why I had never told him. I told him, "I only talk about it if the Holy Spirit tells me to." Then he told me that I stepped out of his beautiful white setting into lush, beautiful green as the Garden of Eden would be. My description falls short of what he described and of his excitement. The "touched by an angel" description is the essence of my story, all to the glory of God.

I left an emotionally traumatized marriage and took my three sons with me. When I left, I knew I was covered by Jesus. I knew I was scripturally covered to go, and through a process, I did. The Holy Spirit also told me there would be problems, but that He would be a husband to the "widow" and a father to the "fatherless." There were lots of problems and He was always there for me.

I was not raised in a church, however, my mother always talked of what was in the Bible. As strange as it sounds, I am now glad that I was not raised in a church. I have never been "indoctrinated." Although doctrine is not all bad, without prior doctrine, I was free and without prejudice to meet the Lord personally and try to do exactly as He told me to do. I never put the Lord in a "box." I didn't know enough to do that. Thus, my wild, intimate ride with the Lord evolved.

The Lord has given me the tongue of the learned. That I should know how to speak a word in season to him that is weary: He awakens me morning by morning; He awakens my ear to hear as the learned.

Isaiah 50:4 (NKJV)

2.

My Letter to Christians

Almost as soon as I dedicated my life to the Lord, the Holy Spirit started impressing me to improve and maintain any physical beauty God had blessed me with. I had joined a Heart to Heart group, and I did the book reviews. I found the book "Fragrance of Beauty."

Most of the encouragement and wisdom in that area came through that book written by Joyce Landorf. Sometimes, I believe we ladies miss some great opportunities for the Lord and for self-fulfillment by not attending to ourselves. To quote Joyce, "If you look good, you feel good. If you feel good, you do good." I believe that includes what you can do for God.

When I read Joyce's book, I was twenty-six years old. I had a six-year old, a four-year old, an infant, and Dawn, my lovely fourteen-year old foster daughter. It would have been quite easy to forget about taking care of myself, especially so because I am a caregiver.

Sometimes under circumstances like I had, and all of us can have, you just get tired. However, at the same time, I had the Lord impressing me to stay as attractive as I could. I also had all these lovely, well-meaning, sincere Christian friends telling me what my "should" and "should nots" were. Don't dance (I love to dance), don't wear makeup. Do this, and don't do that.

I knew very little about the Bible, but one day I said, "Lord, I am confused. I feel you are impressing me in one way and others are telling me the opposite." I opened my Bible and randomly landed in II Kings, second chapter, verse 9. Looking back, I know it wasn't a random choice.

I read the story of Elijah and Elisha. Elisha was taking the mantle of Elijah, who was a prophet of God. He asked Elisha what he could do for him before he went to be with the Lord. Elisha said, "I pray for a double portion of thy spirit on me." By the way, don't ever think God can't do those things now. He is as alive as He has always been.

As a new Christian, I had found what I really wanted, which was a double portion of the Holy Spirit. I also said, "Lord, I have the most wonderful Christian friends in the world, but I ask that you tell me directly what you want me to do and I promise to do it to the best of my ability."

I am, of course, very flawed. I have taken some hard knocks through my own failures, but He has never failed me. I have continued to hear Him and tried to live under His direction.

So, when the Holy Spirit told me to stay physically attractive, that includes the beauty of Jesus shining through us. Beauty counts for nothing if you are ugly inside. When people ask me how I have stayed "young" for my age, I tell them, "Prayer, exercise, vitamins, and whatever sources are available."

In Ms. Landford's book, I believe she directed a lot of information to women so that it would be a benefit to their marriage. So, trying to be a good wife, I vowed to do the best I could with what I had been blessed with. I don't know about the benefits to my marriage as it eventually ended in divorce. Another story. However, God used even that.

Later, the Lord put in my heart to read the story of Esther. Through her beauty, God used Esther to save all her people by being chosen to be the second queen of Xerxes. Read it!!

As time went on, I could look back over the years

and see that during the time I was a single, dancing mom, I had led many dance partners to the Lord. I met many wonderful struggling women and men who would never be in the front pew at church to hear the good news of Jesus Christ. Over many years, I have seen that as my ministry. I am not all that good at working in the church. I go there to stay filled and I preach on the outside in the world. In fact, my brother, Craig, sometimes calls me "Sister Billie." What an honor. I truly believe people feel Jesus in others and that attracts men, women, babies, cats, and dogs.

In synopsis, I truly believe we are commanded to physically take care of our temple. It is where Jesus dwells.

Do you not know that your body is the temple of the Holy Spirit who is in you, whom you have from God, and you are not your own?

Corinthians 6:19 (NKJV)

3.

MIDNIGHT VISITOR

I will start at a time when I was a small child and first felt the Lord's presence. I was maybe six or seven and I was standing by a net fence with morning glories on it. I was studying the beautiful trumpet shaped purple flower and all its intricacies. I suddenly felt a presence beside me and without really knowing God, I knew this was His presence that I was feeling. I believe we are all born with an innate sense of God and we need to watch and listen for His voice.

Sometime later in my bedroom one night, my sister, Connie, and I were sleeping. Suddenly and quietly, I saw a man standing at the end of my bed with moonlight streaming on him though our curtain-less windows. Just touching our covers and then looking out our windows, and then He was back at the end of the bed. I never saw Him leave, but He was soon gone. I was just a little girl and did not say anything. It was not scary, just peaceful, and quiet.

In the morning, I did ask my mom if my beautiful teenage cousin, Tommy, and my young Uncle Larry had come out that night. They sometimes did come by if they had been out together. She said, "No." The knives stuck behind the door frame and across the doors were still there. That was the only way to lock our country home. My parents only locked it because they had one child that would sleepwalk and sometimes go outside.

I was the quiet child of five, and I didn't say anything, but I knew in my heart that my visitor had been Jesus. What I didn't know until many years later, and not until recently, that my sister, Connie, had seen Him too. I was just telling her that story two or three years ago and she in surprise said, "I didn't know you saw Him." We are just one and a half years apart in age, and all through the years, we had never mentioned it. I guess we were both afraid when we were so young that no one would believe us. To this day, I can still see it as if it happened last night.

My father was a good, moral, and hard-working man. He could be fun and loving and he truly loved us. However, he could also get very frustrated. I was a very soft-hearted child. I still am as an adult.

One day, he was being very hard on my precious dog for something I was not even aware of. Being dramatic and hurt, I crawled up on a haystack, threw myself down and said, "God, I want to die." It almost seemed as if the haystack itself spoke and said, "You will never die." I knew once again that I had definitely heard God's voice. Through Christ, we don't die; we merely transition to our new life with Christ.

Then, even as a young girl, I sometimes had dreams that came true. I know God uses that gift from time to time in His children. The first one that I can remember was when I was around nine years old. I dreamed of my mom's best friend, Ruth, having a car accident. In the dream, she had ended up on the lawn of one of her son's coach's house. I told my mother of the dream because I loved Ruth and it upset me.

In the next several days, I learned that the accident happened exactly as I had dreamed it. My mom had told Ruth about my dream and Ruth said, "Please tell Catherine to tell me. Next time, I will be more careful." She was not seriously hurt. However, I had some guilt that I had not warned her. I have never forgotten this dream. It still is sometimes hard for me to tell people what I need to tell them from a dream I have had because they can think I am crazy. I have learned the hard way to do it anyway.

I then began to feel the responsibility of using my gift from God. I was very young. I continued to hear the Lord's voice, but I was quiet and pretty much kept these things to myself. You must remember that I was not living in a practicing Christian home. I really had no one to talk to about such things.

Sometime later, I was going into our only department store in my hometown. It was a small JC Penny's store, and I was on a mission to find new shoes for my county's eighth grade graduation. As I was going into the store, I spotted my uncle Harry's car across the street. At that same moment, the Holy Spirit spoke to me telling me that my uncle Harry and aunt Harlene were pregnant and that they were going to lose the baby.. I did not know that they were pregnant. I somehow knew I was to pray over the baby, and I did so right there on the street. I did not question at all that God had spoken to my heart. So, I prayed and again was quiet. I do remember thinking, *God, why would you ask a twelve-year-old young girl to pray?* I still do not know exactly how all that works, I just know it does. I have no witness to that incident except that of Jesus, but I know I did what He said.

My aunt Harlene had a healthy baby girl and named her Jane. She is a delight and a joy to her mother. They moved away and we did not see the family a great deal. However, when Jane was in college at the University of Nebraska, the Lord gave me a dream that her current boyfriend was not at all good for her. I had never met him but when I called her, she told me that she was realizing that. I was her confirmation. Later, Jane married a wonderful young attorney who is a "Saint."

After the Lord continued to draw me nearer to Him and to be more sensitive to hear Him and do as He impressed me to do, the more carefully I listened, heard, and acted on what He showed me, the more He did that. I think if we all asked, listened, and acted on what we were impressed to do, the more light He would give us to help others.

God impresses things on our heart to make life better, to help others, and to perform His purpose. We are His hands and feet.

When someone is constantly on your mind and heart, call them or go see them before you miss an opportunity or it's too late.

I have people tell me all the time, "'Something' told me not to or to do something." That "something" is the Holy Spirit.

The effective, fervent prayers of a righteous man avails much.

James 5:16 (NKJV)

You are righteous by asking Jesus into your life, and not by being perfect. God certainly knows that I am not. In writing this, it makes me wish I could go back to those childhood days with childlike faith.

4.

Mom and Dad

There is a new song out by Luke Bryan that says in effect that most mothers should be granted sainthood. I believe and I know my siblings believe our mom was one of them.

I have stated before that we were not really raised in a church. We lived on a ranch, five children, not a great deal of money and lots of work to do every day. Our mom had been raised Lutheran and she spoke of things in the Bible, so I had some sparse knowledge.

However, the big however, when I, as a young adult married and with children started to get involved in a church, it was awesome friends from the Nazarene Church and Assembly of God Church that reached out to me. Both churches were of course very foreign to my parents. I now live in the Bible belt, but I grew up in Northern Nebraska. Things were different there. Long story short, I started going to Bible studies and seriously pursuing my Christian life. I was quietly praying, going to church, etc.

One day my parents called and asked me to come out to the ranch because they wanted to talk with me. This was very unusual, but I had two little boys and I thought maybe they were concerned with them, I of course went right out.

They sat me down and proceeded to tell me that they believed I had gone "off the deep end," and things were just not right and that I needed to quit going to these churches, their Bible studies, etc. I was very new in my faith, so it really shattered me and made me worry and doubt myself. I knew in my heart, as hurt and upset as I was, I could not quit. I so felt the Holy Spirit.

It was never mentioned by them again, but the tension hung there somewhat. I cannot fault them because someone saying that God speaks to them can be foreign and as we all know, some people just think it is flat crazy. I persevered.

Fast forward several years, I had moved to Texas. My father had passed, and my mother had been gone maybe a year or so. I had a dream one night of those orange and white cones you see on the highway. I thought maybe that was a sign to be cautious. The next morning, I am barreling down the highway toward Austin, listening to some loud country music (I love country music), and I came upon some orange cones and remembered my dream. I started to slow down and at that exact moment, my mom spoke to me as clearly as if she was in the car. She said, "Catherine, we believe in you." I knew exactly what she was referring to all those years before. They were there in heaven, and now they knew that heaven is real. It was a beautiful sign to me. I cried. I always cry.

If you are faithful in little things, you will be faithful in large ones.

Luke 16:10 (NLT)

5.

PASTOR: THE LAW

Christians, hang onto your hats. This story is rather difficult to write. In fact, I was not going to include it at all. So just read it, and don't judge. It is a story of God's grace and mercy.

I was a young and naïve girl when I married. By the time I had been married to my high school sweetheart thirteen years or so, there had been many indescretions. My self-esteem was at zero. A divorce was already in process and I had dated a nice, kind, and funny guy a few times. However, I was feeling very guilty about that. I was planning on breaking off that dating relationship.

I lived in Nebraska in a small town of less than five hundred people. One Sunday morning, the Holy Spirit put on my heart to go to this small, old Methodist church in this tiny town. Normally, I went to church at the Nazarene church in my hometown, which was ten miles away. However, I knew that I had heard clearly, so I proceeded to go with His voice, and I went to this small church. I had never been inside this church, so I very self-consciously sat down with my youngest son who was maybe six or so. If I remember right, there may have been thirty or thirty-five people in the church. This was a town of five hundred with five churches.

The Pastor, a man maybe in his sixties, gray and balding and not too tall, stood up and said before he gave his sermon, he wanted to explain some things about that sermon. He said that the Holy Spirit had put this sermon on his heart. He also said he would like his wife to come out to verify they had prayed over said sermon and that they were in complete agreement that it was of God.

Now I had never seen this Pastor before, but when his tall, slender wife with creamy skin and beautiful, long, auburn hair came out, I knew of her. She had great credibility with me.

My father had just passed, and this beautiful Pastor's wife had been his nurse. She had always been gracious, helpful, kind, and had asked my siblings and I if she could pray with us. She was a sweet, efficient angel. That is all I knew of her. Now, here she is as the

Pastor's wife. They had evidently moved in recently, as you would generally already know most people in that sparsely populated area.

Then the Pastor with his beautiful, sweet wife beside him said, "I am going to preach on the commandment, 'Thou shalt not commit adultery.'" First of all, I looked around and I was quite literally the only person under eighty. I was in my thirties. My second thought was I am dead.

He, with his wife's blessing, began to preach. The very first thing he said was, "'Thou shalt not commit adultery,' is a huge red light and always will be, do not take it lightly ever."

Second, he preached a sweet, sweet sermon of mercy that in a nutshell was, if you can't love yourself, feel strong in yourself and have no self-worth, you cannot do what you need to do for God; you have nothing to give.

This sweet and strong Pastor based this entire sermon on the fact that the "person" is more important than the law. Don't forget that.

Then, with his wife by his side, he continued with the fact that there is nothing in our human life that takes the place of the relationship of a man and a woman.

There is nothing to replace that, and that relationship is ordained of God.

When the sermon was over, I knew that it was not only okay, but that I should not break up with my kind friend. He was a God send for not only me but for my three sons. He was a good, kind, and athletic guy who was going through some of the same things that I was. One of the most valuable things he told me was, "You have three boys by yourself. You can either run them to athletics or other activities, or you can pay attorneys to keep them out of trouble." I never forgot that. I thank God for good men; they are so practical.

I later took him to church. He struggled but got right with the Lord and at some point, reconciled with his wife and two sons. I later moved to Texas and in the next twenty-five years, we did not talk or see each other at all. I thanked God for his very giving heart, wisdom, and kindness.

Recently, my brother, Craig, who had left Nebraska and moved to Colorado, called me and said, "Cathy, I have a letter from a man in Lincoln, Nebraska that asked me to have you call him. I would have tossed it, but he gave me all your son's names and said he would like to see you all." Yes, it was my friend from years ago. He had, I believe, called somewhere in my hometown, and found my brother's name and address and was trying to find me. He had finished raising his sons and had nursed his wife for years through an early onset of Alzheimer's. She had died several months before and he was reaching to me for comfort and help. He came to visit me at my son's house in Omaha. He had not taken care of his health for years, only his wife's. So, in our two-day visit, I made him a list of things he needed to do. He should have weighed at least one hundred and eighty-five, but he weighed one hundred and forty-five. He was ten years my senior, so I put on that list for him to get a nutritionist, start exercising, working out, and get back on the golf course (his love). Now he was the one who needed the encouragement. I don't see him, but I try to encourage him through phone calls, etc. He has also gone back to church. God is so good. What we reap, we sow, and He brings it around to us.

I did not ever go back to the little church where I heard the sermon that saved me from giving up my love and friend. In fact, I remember just being embarrassed because the Pastor and his wife absolutely had to know who they were preaching to. I did not even thank him. I have prayed that God would bless him for listening. I know he had to listen to God because in his very small, older congregation, preaching that sermon would have made no sense to him at all. Then God brought me where I needed to be to hear that sermon. I could not have made it through without my friend. He was an answer to my prayer.

Even though some things are not God's perfect will, He still uses them all together for good through His love and mercy.

All things work together for good for those who love God, to those who are called according to His purpose.

Romans 8:28 (NKJV)

6.

The Big Brown Car

As I mentioned before, I was a single mom claiming Psalm 68:5 that God is a Father to the fatherless, a defender of "widows" is God in His holy dwelling. I have failed Him, but He has never failed me.

I was living in Terrell, Texas (yes, Jamie Foxx is my friend). On this particular day, my sales career had me in Fort Worth. A miracle in itself that this girl would even attempt to drive in Fort Worth.

It was late afternoon, and suddenly I felt the urgency of the Holy Spirit telling me to go home now. I knew it had something to do with my oldest son, Dale. I rushed as much as I could driving from Fort Worth west of Dallas to Terrell which is east of Dallas.

God's timing is perfect. Just as I pulled into my drive, Dale and his friend, Darren, were just getting into Darren's small convertible. I had a sense in my spirit that something was very wrong. As strange as it sounds, I knew it had something to do with a big brown car!

Darren was taking Dale to work at the Kroger store to stock shelves. I made these two teenagers listen to me telling my "crazy" story about this big brown car. They listened to me with this, "Oh mom, look." but Darren promised me he would be especially careful.

By this time, it was nearly dinner time, so I went to prepare dinner, praying over them all the time. I was thinking, *Why did I let them go?* I remember as I turned from the sink to a counter, I caught a glimpse of something out of the corner of my eye. I turned fully, and it was a very tall angel standing in my small, adjacent living room. I remember its exact color of white and soft shades of gray. It had this peaceful strength, great strength. I knew God sent it to show me my son and Darren had a very protective guardian angel. It seemed as though it was there for minutes, but I am sure it was seconds. I had such a sense of peace. I knew God was in charge of whatever happened, and I was not to worry.

In a little while, my son's friend, Darren, came bursting into the house visibly shaken. He stayed with me until time to pick Dale up from work, which was ten o'clock.

Darren told me this story. He and Dale were going to town on what was a very straight, wide open stretch of two-way highway. He told me that he could see the road was wide open, so he started to pass the dump truck in front of him. However, his car engine "missed," and he remembered what I told him, so he pulled back in behind the dump truck. Just as he pulled back in, the big brown car came barreling by. He said, "I swear there was nothing on that flat straight highway." He knew they most certainly would have had a head-on collision. In his little tin can car they would never have made it.

Darren lived across the country road from us and I hadn't known him long at this time. I just knew he was a very smart, funny, great guy. He still is. He lived with his father who was a professional jockey, and his mother lived elsewhere.

I told Darren again about how the Lord worked that night. I also said, "Darren, I want to go with you to pick up Dale." I drove, and he took me on their previous route. All at once, I began to feel very sick to my stomach. I told him that and he said, "This is right where I went to pass the dump truck." He, by the way, was very incredulous through all of this.

We proceeded on, then when we were pulling into the Kroger parking lot, Darren yelled, "There it is!" The big brown car was coming out. He said, "I remember it had all those stickers on it."

I don't know what all played out that day. My son and I really didn't talk a great deal about it. He knows how I am in the Lord. I truly believed Darren became a believer that night. As far as I knew, his father had no faith, and his mother was a Jehovah's Witness. He did not see her often. God kept all protected and Darren witnessed a miracle through the power of a loving God.

In all your ways, acknowledge Him and He shall direct your paths.

Proverbs 3:6 (NKJV)

7.

THE HITCHHIKER

Wow, where to start! I was driving from Dallas back to Terrell and was nearly out of gas, so I stopped at a gas station in Mesquite, Texas. I started the gas pump and then went inside to get a drink. There, I met John. He was a young, very personable cowboy, whom I assumed was just working there. As we chatted, I soon found out he was, in fact, the owner. No one else was in there at the time, so, as I said, we were just chatting, and somehow the topic turned to chauvinistic men. Then, this sweet, attractive lady walked in. She had heard that last remark about chauvinism, and proceeded to say, "Women do not like chauvinistic men, in fact, they want to open their own doors!" We were all laughing. I soon discovered this feisty lady was John's mother! She then turned to me and said, "Do you like chauvinistic men?" I said, "Of course not, but I do like chivalrous men and I do like doors opened for me." The conversation soon revealed to me John's mom and dad were Pastors. I don't think it was an accident that I stopped at that gas station that day. I believe it was a divine appointment.

This started a very brief "dating" relationship. We went dancing a little and became friends or friendly acquaintances. I would stop for gas if I was over that way. One of my sons even worked for him briefly. I had learned that in my opinion, John was a strong-willed, good guy, that was probably in some rebellion regarding the church. Months went by, occasionally I would stop just to say, "Hi."

At this time, I was working in sales, and one day, I needed to go to Jacksonville, Texas. I had to find it on the map. It was quite some distance southeast of Terrell where I lived. Somehow, I had taken a nice company truck that day instead of my car. I did what I needed to do, and I was outside Jacksonville going back to Terrell. It was late afternoon and I saw a young man hitchhiking. The Holy Spirit said, *'Pick him up.'* I was this little blonde, alone, and I was scared, but I know what I heard, so I pulled up beside him, rolled down the passenger window, and asked him if he wanted a ride. He was very grateful and considerate, he said, "I will just get in the back of the truck." I am thinking, *If God wants me to pick him up, he must want me to talk to him.* I said, "No, get in the front." He probably wondered about me.

In our conversation, he told me his truck broke down on the way home from work. He asked where I lived and I told him Terrell, but I had to return the truck to Mesquite first. He said, "Do you happen to know John Stover?" I laughingly said, "Do you mean John David Stover?" and he said, "Yes."

I knew then there was a reason I had picked up this young man. He quietly pulled out his business card and said, "Would you give him this?" I asked him what I should tell John, and he said, "Nothing, just give it to him." I dropped my hitchhiker off and never saw him again.

God had begun His work and I, to be honest, am still not sure what it was. I went to John's gas station and I explained to John that I had picked up a hitchhiker (I patiently listened to his lecture). Then I told him that I did it at the Holy Spirit's urging. I told him, "The hitchhiker had asked me if I knew you, and that he also asked me to give this card to you." John looked at me a little weirdly!!

I then, of course, handed him the card. He quickly looked up at me and asked again where I got that card.

I patiently reminded him of the hitchhiker the Lord told me to pick up.

Literally, his eyes got big, he turned pale, and started really trembling. As in the proverbial saying, he looked like he had been hit between the eyes.

In my spirit, I knew that not me, not the man whose card I had delivered, but God Himself had struck a chord with John. By the demeanor of both men, I suspected there was a wrong that needed to be made right. John would not tell me anything, so I soon left knowing I had done what I was supposed to do.

This God incident is to remind us God knows and sees everything, even what is in our hearts. We can hide from people, but we cannot hide from God.

But the very hairs of your head are all numbered.
Luke 12:7 (NKJV)

8.

Pearl

I almost don't know how to start my story about Pearl. It is my most touching story. I woke up on a Sunday morning planning to go to church. I lived in Terrell, Texas. My sons were still sleeping, and I was having my first cup of coffee. Suddenly, the Holy Spirit spoke to my heart and said, "Go find the bicycle."

I had a dream right before I woke up that morning. It was of an older craftsman style house that had once been painted white. The outstanding part of the dream was that on the front porch there was a very clean shot of an old, old bicycle the likes of which I had never seen and I had seen some as my dad was an auctioneer that did estate sales. Also, in this dream was a very distraught mother worrying about her "boy." I said, "Lord, I don't recognize that house at all." He said, "Just get in your car, I will lead you."

I got out of my PJ's, got in my car, and just said,

"Okay, I am listening." I remember sitting there thinking, *Have I lost it?* The Holy Spirit led me from my home on Grace Lane to the complete opposite end of town. I just turned where I felt led to turn. It took me about twenty minutes.

I came to realize I was in a part of town that pizza places were refusing to deliver to because they would be robbed during deliveries. However, I kept going. I turned a final corner, and there directly in front of me, was the old house with "the bicycle," exactly as I had dreamed it. Once I saw that bicycle, I knew I was supposed to go in and tell some lady something about what I thought was her little boy. Moms always think their sons are their little boys!

I was sitting in my car, still afraid to go in. Then, some clean-cut man walked out and got in his very nice, white truck. That gave me some comfort, so I said, "Okay Lord, here goes."

I very timidly walked up and knocked on a screen door. Still checking over my shoulder all the while. Some lady (Pearl) asked me what I wanted. She was afraid and sounded kind of rough. All I could say was, "Ma'am, do you have a son? The Lord sent me here to talk to you about your son." I, of course, still don't have a clue what I am supposed to tell her about her son. However, she said, "Come in, I am Pearl."

Pearl laid on a bed in the living room with a long, ominous-looking pistol beside her. I was hoping she liked me! She told me the week before an eighty-four-year-old woman across the street had been raped. I had heard that on the news. That's why she had the gun there.

Still, not knowing what I was supposed to tell her, I said, "Pearl, do you have a son?" She said, "Yes." and began to cry and pour her heart out to me. Her son, and only child, was in the military and in harm's way. However, what she was most worried about was that he might be killed and not make it into heaven because he was living a very carnal lifestyle; smoking, drinking, and all that sometimes goes with a partying lifestyle of a young man. She said, "I raised him in the church, and he knows the Lord, but he is living a worldly life."

The Holy Spirit began to tell me what to say to this very distraught mother; that He knew her son, He was protecting her son and she was not to worry over him, that God had him in the palm of His hand.

I had to tell her over and over and over again how I got there and why God sent me. I am sure that it was difficult to grasp since I seemed to have come from nowhere, and she did not know who I was.

She finally seemed to grasp that I was strictly a messenger, but I had to have come through the bidding of the Holy Spirit. She had been begging God for comfort and He had been faithful! That comfort just came in a different way than she was expecting. She did seem to finally get that!

Pearl couldn't get out of bed, but she asked me to go into the hall to see her son's picture and to pray for him. I walked through this very, very sparsely furnished house with layers of newspaper on the floor for insulation. I was broken-hearted that she was living trapped in a bed with almost nothing. This beautiful, praying saint was asking for one thing only: prayers for her son.

We prayed together and I assured her one more time that God had her son as in Psalm 91. He has sent me there to tell her so, and except for God's miracle, I would not know her at all.

When she was finally assured that God knew her son and loved him just as he was, I left and went to my car and cried as I always do. Tears of joy at the awesomeness of God and how much trouble He went through just to comfort one saint lying in bed with a gun beside her for protection and newspapers on the floor for insulation. I still cannot read this story without tears of sadness for Pearl's physical situation and tears of joy for God's love and goodness to her.

I always get through these God appointments strongly and then, like I said, when I leave, I melt into tears for the awesomeness of God. In this case, I was very overcome and did not think to take the address. I tried four or five times to find her and take her food or something, but I never could locate her again.

I had to finally just believe God did not want me "hanging out" in that area and maybe delivering food was the assignment of the man that went before me.

"He who dwells in the shelter of the most high will rest in the shadow of the Almighty.

I will say of the Lord, "He is my refuge and my fortress. My God in whom I trust."

Psalm 91:1 (NIV

9.

BILL

I had been in Texas for several years, living in Terrell, Texas. One Friday night, I came home after a long week of work at the law office, helping with schoolwork for three boys, doing laundry, etc., you know the routine. I was tired and rarely did anything on Friday nights except rest and relax. This night though, the boys were either out with friends or spending the night with friends.

By 9:30 p.m. or so, I had just crawled into bed. The Holy Spirit said, *"Get up and go to Lee's Silver Fox,"* which was a country dance place not far from my home. I hate to admit that I groaned and complained a little, maybe a lot. I was so very tired, and although I knew I would have friends there, Marilyn, one of my teacher friends in particular, I still hated to walk in anywhere alone.

Nevertheless, with a wrong attitude, I threw on a

little makeup, put on my boots and white dress and went to Lee's.

I danced a couple of times, then sat down with some friends and immediately, this tall, dark curly-haired handsome young man came and asked me to dance. He was probably ten years younger than I. We danced a couple of times, not country style as I learned later, he was from California. He told me his name was Bill and then he proceeded to tell me something no one else ever had. He told me that he asked me to dance because when he saw me dancing with someone else earlier, that there was a white aura all around me. Yes, he was perfectly sober, and yes, I promptly dropped my grumpy, feeling sorry for myself, I am tired attitude. I knew this is exactly why God said, "*Go to Lee's Silver Fox.*"

Bill was staying with an aunt and uncle in Terrell. After that night, he always wanted to spend time with me. However, I was working full-time and a single mom and all that goes with that, so I didn't have a great deal of time. One summer's evening, Bill called and asked me to go to a movie. I said, "Bill, I can't. I am going to a Friday night Bible study." He asked, "Can I go with you?" How do you say no to that?

I picked him up at his aunt and uncle's house and we went to the Reagan's home to the Bible study. I got to the door and my missionary friend, Jacque, opened the door and said, "We don't need any…," laughing as only Jacque can laugh, loudly and full of joy and music. Bill looked at me and said, "I have not heard laughter for so long." That remark really stunned me, as our group was always laughing. That night, he was very open to share his personal story with the group. He was visiting his aunt and uncle who were very good people. However, he has been living in California, where evidently, his entire family, including his parents, were living in a very dark world of drugs, drug parties, and no laughter.

That night, the host of the party, Mr. Reagan, Jacque's husband, Sam, Jerry Kines, and some other wonderful Christian men asked him if he would like to give his life to the Lord. He said, "Yes" immediately, and they took him into their kitchen and led him to the Lord.

I cry as I write this and think I grumbled about getting out of bed and going to Lee's Silver Fox. Again, God does not use me because of who I am, but in spite of who I am.

Bill continued to spend time with me and with my friends. However, he soon went back to California. Without a support group, he went back to his dysfunctional family and attended a drug party. He was sitting on a couch beside his best friend when that friend decided to play Russian Roulette with a pistol. The first shot killed his friend. Bill called me devastated and he moved immediately to one of the Carolinas with a family member that lived a more appropriate lifestyle. That ended his previous lifestyle.

I don't know all the logistics, but Bill called me from Oklahoma and wanted me to join him. He played guitar and sang and had started making videos and visiting schools to educate elementary school children about the dangers of drugs. I so hope he has stayed on that path. It was not, of course, God's will for me to join him, but I continue to pray for him.

Please, if God puts something on your heart, do it now. Even a phone call can change a life for the Lord. Try not to grumble like I did that night as I drug my tired body out of bed to go dancing.

And let us not grow weary in well-doing, for in due time we will reap if we do not give up.

Galatians 6:9 (NKJV)

10.

Gregory

I always try to remember the Lord uses me only because of who I am in Him. When I think of the experiences I have had in the Lord, this is a very special, vivid one.

As I stated previously, I was a struggling single mom. My youngest son, Justin Burr, was working at a local restaurant owned by a wonderful lady named Virginia, who was the grandmother of his best friend, Lance.

One night, I felt led to take my two older sons, Dale and Clint, out to eat at this restaurant. I assumed that was so we could see Justin Burr and spend some family time together.

However, as we entered the restaurant, there was a table on the left with five or six men at it, all of whom looked as if they had just gotten off work. As we walked by, we said, "Hi," but the Holy Spirit quickened me to chat a minute. Much to protective Dale's horror, and my Clint's, "Are you sure that's appropriate attitude, mom?" Such good sons! I did linger a minute.

As I visited with them, the Lord spoke a word of knowledge to my heart. That word was, *"Celebrity."* Remember that little side note.

Through the conversation, and really that conversation was with one man, Gregory, who was clearly the leader of the group. We visited a little, and my sons and I moved on.

In the coming days, when I would go to pick up my son from work, this same group of men would be there. It seems they were staying at the hotel close by and that is where they ate dinner every night.

Since the restaurant was owned by friends, I had often come in for coffee or dessert while waiting for my son to get off work. Eventually, as I got to visit with Gregory, we became friends and he asked me to go to a picnic with him. Remember the side note, "Celebrity?" The picnic was at Mickey Gilley's home in Pasadena! He certainly qualifies as a celebrity, especially in Texas. There was a very large dance hall across the highway from the restaurant, so it was not unusual to know of some of the country music stars.

However, in this case, it was my confirmation that I had "heard" correctly when I first felt led to stop and visit a minute.

I did not go to that picnic because it did not feel appropriate to do so. I also, of course, did not like leaving my three sons overnight because I had no support system at all.

After a few weeks, Gregory asked me to go dancing at the place across the street. However, the night before that date, I had a very vivid dream of a funeral. This funeral was very beautiful. The casket was a soft silver, the flowers were sweetheart roses with white baby's breath. I didn't know whose funeral it was, however, I knew this was definitely a funeral that was very feminine. The other distinct thing regarding this funeral was there were seven nice looking men around the casket. Gregory was also very nice looking.

There was a distinct variation in their ages. In my dream, I thought they ranged from twenty-five to fifty or so. It was such a vivid dream; it was as if I was there at the funeral. I knew this dream had something to do with Gregory. He was not, however, one of the men I "saw" at the funeral.

We went on this "date," and all I could think about

when I looked at him was of this dream of a feminine funeral. This is a first date, I barely know him, and I am not very bold, so it was hard for me to approach the subject of a dream about a funeral.

At this point, I am thinking that maybe it is a warning for some woman in his life. So, of course, I am trying to think how I can get my message across to him without him thinking I am totally crazy.

Finally, I said something like, "Gregory, do you have a sister?" He said, "No, I just have seven brothers!" I casually asked, "How old are your brothers?" He told me they ranged from twenty-five to fifty-two. Now I know without a doubt this is a dream from God. These are the men I "saw" at the funeral.

I did not tell him of the dream that night. I did, however, continue to be concerned about the death of a woman in his life. I tried again and said, "You should call your mom and check on her." He assured me he had just talked to her and she was fine. I am sure he is thinking, *Why is this woman concerned about my mom?*

I am all this time praying. Lord, *Where do I go with this?* It always feels like a huge responsibility on my shoulders and I am hitting a brick wall. All the time thinking, *I am not very good at this, Lord.*

We had a few more "dates." I asked him to go to church. He wanted to go to his denomination, so we did. That did tell me he was a believer. He was a quiet, reserved guy and I am kind of the same way, so it was not exactly easy to tell him of my concerns. I just assumed he would think I was "a little off."

Finally, one night as I was getting out of his car, I just sat back and said, "I have something to tell you." I very carefully told him the details of the beautiful, feminine funeral with the seven men around the casket, and also of my fears for some woman in his life. He listened carefully, showing no emotion, and making no comment. Completely closed off from me. I said, "I am so sorry, but I just had to tell you what God showed me." I thought to myself, *I will never see him again.* It was for sure not a normal date.

Strangely enough, he started to do more things for me. He made an effort to do very nice things for my youngest son, who he had gotten to know through the restaurant when I was not around. Neither of us ever mentioned my dream again. I just felt I had done what I was supposed to do. Perhaps a couple months passed, I am not sure exactly how long it was.

Then one night, at about midnight, he called me. He was crying and very upset. Not reserved at all now but pouring out his heart to me. He told me the dream I had of a funeral was of his high school sweetheart. I believe they were engaged.

The story was one we hear often. After graduation or prom, I can't remember which, they had gone to a party, and at some point, they had an accident. His sweetheart was killed, and he was hurt so badly he could not attend her funeral. That is why I did not see him there at the funeral in my dream. All those years of guilt and pain came pouring out of this kind, reserved man.

This night, he had just had a dream of that accident, and as he got out of his car and went around to open the passenger door, instead of finding his sweetheart dead, I stepped out and I was smiling.

In his flood of emotion, he said he knew God was giving him a second chance through me. Strangely, his sweetheart and I had the same name.

I knew I was in his life only to lead him out of his great burden of guilt and shame. The Holy Spirit began to give me the words he needed to hear; that his sweetheart was with Jesus in His loving arms and that no one could love her more.

He was to be assured we only see through dark glasses and one day we would see all was right with the Lord and that he was forgiven—totally.

Eventually, the Holy Spirit urged me to tell Gregory that what He wanted of him was to go on and live out the purpose that God had for Gregory here on Earth, that he was covered by the blood and He expected him to carry out His purpose.

I saw Gregory for some time after that and I assured him we were not to be together as a couple, that I was just God's instrument to be used in his life, that God had his past in His hands and he was covered by the blood. He soon finished his work and left.

Sometime later, I received a nice thank you letter from Him telling me he had the perfect wife for him, and they had a baby on the way.

Yes, I was still there raising my three sons the best I knew how to. I loved it! Fine sons they are.

For as the heavens are higher than Earth, so are my ways higher than your ways and my thoughts higher than your thoughts.

Isaiah 55:9 (NIV)

11.

THE APPLEBEE'S ANGEL

Let me preface this miraculous encounter by saying when my youngest son was in college, I married again. We will call him JT. He was a successful, smart, accomplished man, but not always forthright.

One evening I was going to meet two of my dear friends at Applebee's for a salad. One of my friend's name was Sharon. She is a beautiful, extremely talented, Christian musician, and my other Christian friend was Patty.

I was the first to arrive and I was sitting in a booth by myself, close to the front entrance. As I sat there, I did notice a crisply dressed cowboy at another table glancing at me. I really thought very little of that. Soon, Patty and Sharon came in, we talked and laughed, then settled in our booth.

Within minutes, the cowboy that had sent glances my way was at the end of our booth. He profoundly stated, "I am Dale, I need to talk to you girls." I am still kind of laughing with the girls, however, since I have done exactly what he was doing, and since he had waited to come to the booth after my friends arrived, I said, "Okay."

Patty and Sharon had slipped into the seats opposite of me, so I invited him to sit down beside me. I was, to be honest, still wondering if he was flirting or what. Since he had not approached me when I was alone, and because of his serious demeanor, I thought him to be sincere.

Nevertheless, I was still being rather light-hearted. I laughingly said, "These are my friends, Sharon and Patty, and I am 'Katrina.'" He looked me directly in the eye and said, "No, you're Catherine." He now had my full attention. I had never seen him before.

Patty will tell you herself, she is the very cautious, practical one of the three. She was still, rightfully scrutinizing our new friend. Like he had to me, he turned to her and said, "You need to not judge me."

Although I cannot recall every detail, he proceeded to tell her that she may need to take over more responsibility than she had at the time. Her sweet husband had cancer earlier, and a heart condition.

Then, Dale turned to Sharon and continued his astounding synopsis of the wonderful things she had done, and a couple she may need to change. Again, all three witnesses knew every word he said was the truth.

Then, Dale turned to me, addressing me by my correct name and very surprisingly told me something very unspiritual! He said I needed to be checking credit cards and bank accounts, something that is definitely not part of my nature. He continued by saying, "Do not do anything, he will do it." I did not know what that meant at the time. He finished telling me what to do, looked at all of us, and said, "You will never see me again." We, of course, watched him walk out, get in a white Jeep, and drive off. We sat there stunned, and Patty said, "Was he an angel?"

Neither of his statements about bank accounts would have made any sense, except that just one day prior to this encounter, I had an incident with a check. Patty's daughter had been babysitting for my very young granddaughter. As I was driving Patty's daughter home after babysitting, she said to my granddaughter, "I want to show you my room."

I was tired so I was thinking, *Oh good, I will take a break in my car.* Good idea, however, the Holy Spirit spoke to my heart and said, "*Go in.*" I did so, and to my surprise, Patty's husband was at home laying on the couch as he was not feeling well. He was one of JT's golf partners and a sweetheart of a guy, so, of course, he sat up to visit with me. As he did so, he picked up a check that was lying on the end table by the couch. He handed it to me and said, "Look what your silly husband did!" My husband worked out of town all week and I lived in a suburb of Austin where we had built a home for someday retirement. That was his idea, by the way.

I took the check and he proceeded to tell me, "He sent me this $3.00 check to pay a golf bet from when he was home last weekend." I just did not think, I blurted out, "I didn't know we had an account at that bank." My poor friend felt badly and so did I for putting him in a bad spot!

I had not seen Patty then, nor had I said anything to her about the check incident. Now here is a stranger telling me to check our bank accounts. Patty's eyes quickly darted towards me. I knew she knew about the previous day.

The following day after our "angel's" sage advice, I went to the out of town bank that check was written on, gave the teller my ID and said, "I would like to check our balance."

She came back, a little shaken, and said, "I am sorry, I can't give you that balance, he is a single man." Surprising how intelligent and knowledgeable our angel was.

I never mentioned the check incident to my then husband, however, I knew by his guilty demeanor when he came home that weekend, that he had gotten an apology call from our friend, letting him know he had thrown him under the proverbial bus.

There were more incidents regarding calls from credit card companies for unsavory charges on our joint card, and then on another card I didn't know existed.

Long story short, the Applebee's angel was definitely right about Sharon, Patty, and I.

Ultimately, JT asked for a divorce. Without that angel, because I was so naïve, I probably would not have survived the difficulty that would have followed.

I needed to know what God already knew. He miraculously took care of me through His messenger. I never did have to do anything except sign papers.

God sees all and protects His own.

He said to them, "You are the ones who justify yourselves in the eyes of others, but God knows your hearts."
Luke 16:15 (NIV)

12.

Radioactive

I was a Dolly Parton naturally, as were my three sisters. I am not talking about the singing part!

A while after I had three children and was in my thirties, I started having back problems from lack of support for my huge "blessings." I was quite small framed so I sought out a cosmetic surgeon and had a breast reduction, which by the way, was one of the best things I have ever done for myself.

Fast forward several years, and the Holy Spirit spoke to me to have another reduction! I really thought, *This can't be God, I am just fine.*

I always ask for three confirmations, and I received them. So, finally I called my Christian friend and cosmetic surgeon, Dr. Fred Wilder in Austin, Texas. He is very conservative and I trust him completely, so when he said, "It's been some time, so I do think I can help you some with continued support," I said, "Okay, let's do it." I heal very quickly and with very little or no scarring, so I was not concerned at all about the surgery.

However, I did have one concern. I had just met a really nice, Christian man and I thought, *This is embarrassing. I am going to have to tell him because we were seeing each other nearly every day.* I told him what I felt the Lord was impressing me to do. In true form he said, "If this is what you believe you should do, I will help take care of you." He did.

All went well with the surgery. I was in the hospital just one night. My doctor told me to come back in six weeks for a follow-up visit. In less than three days, Mitsy, his sweet coordinator called me and said, "Cathy, Dr. Wilder would like to see you as soon as possible." My antenna went up immediately, of course. I said, "Mitsy, what happened to six weeks?" She said, "I am not going to lie, there is a reason for concern." My heart dropped and I went in as soon as I could. When my doctor came in, he looked so sad and upset. Then he said the words every woman dreads; "Cathy, after a reduction, the tissue that is removed has to be sent to a lab for testing. Those tests show that you have breast cancer in the left breast. It isn't a bad actor, but we have no way of knowing exactly where the tissue came from." He said this had only happened one other time in his twenty-five years of practice.

He was so apologetic that I told him that God had impressed me to have this surgery and that I was sure he had actually helped me.

He also told me his mother had just died of breast cancer, so he knew all the best doctors to send me to. I loved them. The surgeon that did a lumpectomy said, "Not that I am not a good doctor, but could I pray with you?" I loved that. God always has the right people at the right time.

Eventually, I found out the cancer was in, what they called, "Stage 0-1." It was determined that I should start with radiation, thirty-seven treatments administered on a daily basis.

I started radiation and, God being God, had placed a beautiful red-haired Christian lady named Olivia at the front desk of the treatment area. She prayed with me from the first day on. God does place his angels.

The first day of radiation was no problem, quick and easy. On the second day as I was turning into the hospital, I saw a vision of a man's face in front of me. No, I did not freak out and crash. He had gray hair, a rather heavy mustache, and he was slightly burly looking.

True to form for our God, when I sat down there was the man sitting at a right angle to me. I said, "Okay God, here we go."

I spoke to him and asked him how he was doing with treatment. I will call him Mark. Mark had an opening in his throat, so it was obvious he had throat cancer. He told me when he took radiation, he did okay, but when he had chemo, he was violently ill and could not do anything for days. He was a single father and his young adult son lived with him, so it was very difficult. He was a truck driver and he also could not drive after chemo.

Remembering, of course, my vision of him, I said, "Well sir, may I pray for you?" To which he replied rather harshly, "I don't believe in all that garbage." Hmmm… I had my work cut out for me. I just smiled at him. Then he said, "Well, you can pray if you want to, I don't care."

Immediately and discreetly, I asked Olivia, my Christian prayer partner at the front desk to pray for him and for me.

Mark and I saw each other many times over the next five weeks as our daily appointments were back to back. I wonder who arranged that long ago. We talked nearly every day and I, at times, gently, very gently, talked about my faith.

Then one day he said, "It's time for my chemo, I so dread it." I just quietly told him I would pray that he would not get sick this time. He did not comment at all.

I didn't see him for several days, however, the next time he came in he came over to me and began to tell me that when he got home from chemo this time, he felt great. He cleaned his entire house, cooked, and went out with his son and was never sick one time.

I could tell by his demeanor he was still in awe and excited. Then he started saying, "Well, I still don't really believe," at which time I jumped up, firmly tapped him on the chest, and said, "Don't give me that." For some reason, I was kind of mad. I proceeded to say, "You know without a doubt that was totally God." He looked very shocked at my boldness and I was most certainly looking up at this big guy. Then he said, "You are probably right." To which I replied, "You know you are a believer, and you know I am right."

I told him then of my vision of him and that God had asked me to pray for him. I think the poor man was a little overwhelmed at this point and was trying to process all that I had just told him. That was my last treatment and I assured Mark I would keep praying for him. Although I never saw him again, that is not the end of this story.

I had a wonderfully kind breast cancer specialist, Dr. Owen Winsett, through all of this ordeal. Standard procedure would have been for me to have more treatments such as hormone stripping. However, every time he suggested another treatment, the Holy Spirit would give me a definite no. That was a little scary for me to go against a fine doctor's recommendations. Quite frankly, it doesn't really please doctors either! Every six months he would try to convince me to take more treatments. I still got a spiritual no.

A few years later, the same doctor sat me down and told me that what I had at the time is no longer considered cancer. They do not treat it at all.

I truly believe God had me go through all of that for the soul of one precious man.

When you go through a storm, and it was a storm for me, trust God. He has allowed that storm and has a plan for you, and maybe more importantly, as in this case, for someone else. He did not have to impress me to go for that reduction. He was in total control and had a plan. I have been completely blessed by the entire episode.

We know that all things work together for good to those who love God, to those who are called according to His purpose.

Roman 8:28 (NKJV)

13.

JUNE

I was in the middle of a remodel. There was the sound of hammers and even jack hammers all over the house. Not to mention, the painters and electricians. These guys also always have lively music in the background.

Even with all the chaos, I suddenly became very sleepy. I crept into a dust-covered guest bedroom for a power nap, which I am famous for. That nap found me dreaming about a lady with sandy-brown hair done in a very distinct hairstyle. The unique hairstyle is what really was prominent in my dream. I know, strange. In this dream, I knew I was to talk to her. That was it, that's all I knew.

I got up, went back to work, but of course, I never forgot the dream. Generally, I write my dreams down in as much detail as possible. I have learned that when God gives me a dream, I need to watch, and He will present the opportunity. I need to fulfill the purpose of that dream.

In a week or two, I told Warren, the kind Christian man I was dating, we need to go eat at Wildfire tonight. Our favorite restaurant in Georgetown, Texas. It still is. We have never had bad food or service there. However, on this particular night, first of all, it was like we were invisible! No one would wait on us. Then, we finally got our drink order in and it was wrong. This continued with slow service, wrong food, and on and on. Frankly, we were getting impatient. Finally, as we were leaving our cozy little booth, I headed for the door, and just coming in, was the lady with the unique hairstyle. With her, was a very attractive dark-haired girlfriend. I was surprised but kept going. I was thinking, *How do I tell Warren I need to go back and talk to a stranger?*

Nevertheless, "something" stopped me. Don't we always say, "something" told me, when we really know it's the Holy Spirit? I simply told him I had a dream about that woman, and I need to talk to her. He quickly answered, "That sounds like God, let's go back."

I went back in, and she and her friend were standing, waiting for a table. At this point, I have no idea what I am supposed to tell her. Nevertheless, I walk up to her and say, "Miss, I need to talk to you. God gave me a dream about you." Then, the Holy Spirit started telling me what to say to her.

I asked her, "Have you made a decision today? God is very proud of you for that decision. He wants you to remember that decision and cling to it when things get hard. Again, He is very proud of you."

She, of course, looks rather confused. She grabbed my hands, and then she asked me a strange question. She asked, "Do you know me from the White House?" I said, "Honey, I have never been to the White House." Again, she said, "You must know me from the White House." I told her one more time, "I have never met you, I just dreamed about you, and I am just here to tell you God loves you and is so very proud of you for the decision you have made." She started to cry. Her attractive friend had been listening intently, and she entered the conversation. She said, "June did just make a decision tonight. The White House is where Alcoholics Anonymous meets. Tonight, she has made the decision to give up alcohol."

Finally, it all made sense to me. I reminded her again that God saw her make that decision and He loved her and was there for her. Her friend assured me that she was her sponsor and that she would not let her forget.

It always amazes me that God never gives me the words until I need them. I just have to trust Him. Remember all those delays at the restaurant with our food and drinks? God's timing is always perfect.

I then left the restaurant with Warren who always supports me in these things. I left and I cried, I always cry to see the awesomeness of God's love for one struggling little lady. I am always so truly humbled when He uses me in this way. Just remember He uses us all in different ways, and He uses me, not because of who I am, but because of who I am in Him.

For the Lord gives wisdom; from His mouth comes knowledge and understanding.

Proverbs 2:6 (NIV)

14.

Prison

Foolishly, when I was first divorced, I believed I could get up at 5:00 a.m., go to bed at midnight, go to work, go to college, and raise three sons and all that goes with that. I was keeping those hours at the time this story took place. I was a little tired!

However, on this particular morning, I had just taken my sons to each of their three separate schools and I was on my way to my job at the University of Nebraska Law College. It was a cold wintry day with freezing rain on the streets. I was coming down a small hill in Lincoln praying I would not slide down this particular hill!

I was contemplating a dream I had right before I woke up. Many times, if it's a dream with a purpose from God, I will have that dream right before I wake up. That is probably so I will remember it!

On this very early morning, I had a dream of a

young man, tall, slender, and dressed in all denim. He was walking down the street, and just as I noticed him in this dream, he flipped around and a rather large, silver cross on a chain around his quite bare chest flipped out. He had his thumb in the air.

It seemed as though I had barely had these thoughts of my dream. When just less than a half-block ahead of me, this young man was flipping around with his cross flying out and his thumb in the air. This scene was playing out in front of me exactly as my dream was.

My first thought was, *It's icy and I am afraid to try and stop on this street.* I had begun praying I would make it to work without an accident. My second fleeting thought was, *This is a hitchhiker.* Always a little scary for a young woman alone.

Of course, the cross won out, it always does! I stopped and asked this bare-chested young man if he needed a ride. He got in rather quickly as his denim jacket and no shirt were no match for the cold.

I asked him where he was going, and he said to the state prison to see his dad. I was early for work and it wasn't far. Not to mention, this was a God assignment. So of course, I said, "Okay." I turned around and headed for the prison.

I proceeded to tell him I liked his cross and I asked him if he was a Christian (not everyone wearing a cross is, by the way).

He was very open and very matter-of-factly told me some friends had just, in the last several days, led him to the Lord. He was on his way to the prison to tell his dad the good news and to share Jesus with him. I was a little shocked at his frankness.

Now, when I was a new Christian, I was very timid, shy, and maybe even afraid to share my faith with anyone. This young man was not wasting any time. I was, in fact, a little ashamed of myself!

This is not just a story of a ride to prison for a young man on a mission. My stopping for him and sharing my dream with and of him was a confirmation to him that God had seen his commitment and He was there for him.

I took him to the prison and told him I could wait for him. I knew if I called the Law College, my longtime friend, Don Shaneyfelt, the acting Dean of the College, and certainly my Christian boss, Janet Krause, Dean of Psychology, would understand. He assured me he already had a ride home; he had just not had a way to the prison.

I prayed for him, dropped him off, and went on my merry way to work. I was feeling very, very blessed to be part of a plan from a God who loves us so much. He is just waiting for us to come to Him.

Seek His will in all you do, and He will show you which path to take.

Proverbs 3:6 (NLT)

It Started With a Dream

~

Finding Your Dream

OG Mandino, one of my favorite authors, has a vow, it is: "I promise... I swear... I vow... to never forget the greatest talent God has bestowed on me is the power to pray." Remember his vow!

The Prayer, by Andrea Bocelli and Celine Dion is my favorite song. Listen to it!

It doesn't matter where you are in your life right now... find your dream. My story is very evident in this book. Your story may be that of a highly successful businessperson, teacher, actor, or counselor.

There is only one of you in this world. Find your calling. There are three simple steps to achieving your story. They are as follows: Pray, listen, and act. Use your God-given instincts.

This morning, I was walking Theo. My little six-pound black and white yorkie started to eat something left by a construction worker. I quickly pulled him back because I know what is good for him. Now, God doesn't have a leash on us, we have our own free will. However, if we listen, we will be so much more in God's will, which is good for us, and definitely for others. You can learn to hear God in detail if you listen and stay in His word.

BIOGRAPHY

Catherine Lambley Scott

From humble beginnings as a child, from struggles in her adult life, that at times were devastating to her and her children, she has risen above it all. How did she do it, you ask? She did it with a strong backbone, an internal, emotional sensitivity, and her determination to listen to the Holy Spirit. From these virtues, she never wavered.

Unconditional love and support for family, friends, and unknown others regardless of their differences is but one of her strengths. The ability to unashamedly write from her heart about truthful experiences is a gift to many.

Carol Lambley Huffman

CPSIA information can be obtained
at www.ICGtesting.com
Printed in the USA
LVHW012325210221
679514LV00007B/964